YOUNG ING

A Guide to Staying Young Forever

ISBN-10: 0-9825701-0-4

EAN13: 978-0-9825701-0-4

Formatting and illustrations by

Kathrine Rend :: Rend Graphics 2009

www.rendgraphics.com

Published by:

LIMERIX PRESS

www.LimerixPress.com

To order additional copies, please visit:

www.amazon.com

Dedication

This book is lovingly dedicated to Evelyn Katz, without whose devotion to whimsy and staying young, this book would never have been written. But I jest! I sincerely dedicate it to:

Kat Rend who caught the spirit of Young Ing in her exquisite illustrations.

Moe Katz, her husband for his constant encouragement and deep pockets.

Roger Katz, her son, for literally keeping her on the beat.

Karen Katz, her daughter-in-law for suggesting Young Ing be illustrated.

Grace Skinner, her sister, for encouraging her to go on to verse 2 after having been sent verse 1 on a lark.

You, dear reader, for taking Young Ing in the spirit in which it was written!

Thank you.

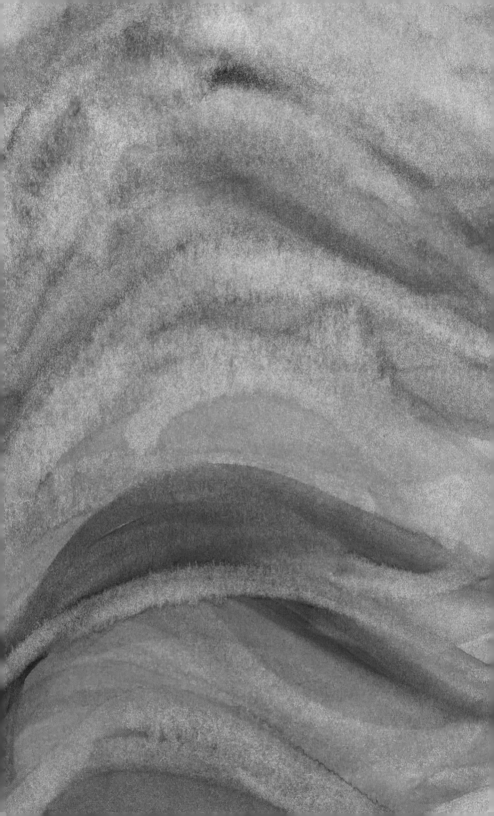

There was an old person called Ing
Whose age was a worrisome thing.
A good one she found.
She turned hers around
And now she's the happy Young Ing!

No one could believe such a thing
Could be said of decrepit old Ing.
"Hey, how can that be?
Old Ing's 93!"
"I'm 39 now!" said Young Ing.

The word on Young Ing was now out.
To see what the fuss was about
They came with delight
To view this rare sight
And left her with nary a doubt.

Reporters got hold of the story
And seeking to boost their own glory,
They put her on telly
And featured her belly
—A welcome relief from the gory!

The #1 question was how?
They wanted to find out right now!
Those wrinkles all lost!
How much had it cost?
What doctor was taking a bow?

"I did it myself!" said Young Ing.
"No doctors! No botox!
NO NOTHING!
It cost not a penny!
The pleasures are many!
I've never been more full of zing!"

My name's not Young Ing just by chance.
I wanted my life to enhance.
So here is my story:
For folly or glory.
No matter. I'm doing a dance!

I'll tell you how things worked for me.
To find a good age was the key.
If you pick one too young
You won't get it done
'Cuz your doubts will win out, don't you see?

So how can you find a good age
That jets you right out of your cage
That makes you feel good
Like everyone should
And into the next wacky stage?

You might want to simply reverse
The actual numbers you curse.
To do that is cool.
It follows a rule.
There's many a way would be worse.

In choosing an age just remember
That old can feel cold, like December.
It could make you feel
That you've lost your zeal
—A fire all burned but the ember.

So think not of winter, but spring
A green May or June is the thing.
Pick one that excites you
And surely invites you
To dance a wild dance and to sing!

My age choice was quite a big leap.
I'd thought of the outcomes I'd reap.
What mental debates!
No more senior rates.
Was *that* worth my old age to keep?

For me the choice was a no-brainer.
I'd already hired a trainer
To shape up my bod
To be sleek like a rod
That made me feel saner and saner!

If you want to get young on the cheap
A few wrinkles you may want to keep
It's all up to you
Whatever you do.
While you ponder, your thoughts may run deep.

So here is the yin and the yang
Think old and you just feel a pang.
So it's good to know
Think young—you let go
—that song of old age that you sang.

That song is the boring refrain
That gives us all such a big pain
That makes us feel stuck,
Bogged down in deep muck
—Of all our existence the bane!

And now I will give you the key
To get where you're wanting to be.
The key is feel good .
I now understood!
So *feel good* is what worked for me.

The thing that was hardest to learn
(It had been my biggest concern):
To put others first
Would just be the worst.
I now had to make a U-turn.

I had to discover a way
To not give a rip what they say.
So *my* biggest deal
Was care how *I* feel
And learn how to do that each day.

"But isn't that selfish?" you ask:
"If in your own pleasures you bask?
Since I was a tot
I've never forgot
PLEASE OTHERS to be my main task!"

That may have been what you were taught
But look from that what you have got:
It's never enough!
Your skin looking rough
Despite all the creams you have bought!

If happy is selfish, so what?
You want to get out of your rut.
You want a new age
But fear there'll be rage
To follow the voice of your gut!

"It seems not that easy to do.
They could be upset if they knew.
If I did the wrong thing.
Tell me, Young Ing
How I could get out of *that* stew."

That's just what's in need of removal
Your seeking for others' approval!
There's just *you* to please
With fun and with ease
So think of yourself as a jewel!

And though it may cause quite a stink
Don't fret about what THEY may think.
It's all how you feel-
A very big deal!
It could be that long-missing link.

Let's just put this thing to the test.
For one week do what you love best.
You're bound to feel good
Like everyone should!
Elated and bubbling with zest!

If after the end of that time
Your feelings don't touch the sublime
With transports of joy
Like a kid with a toy!
So what? Is it that big a crime?

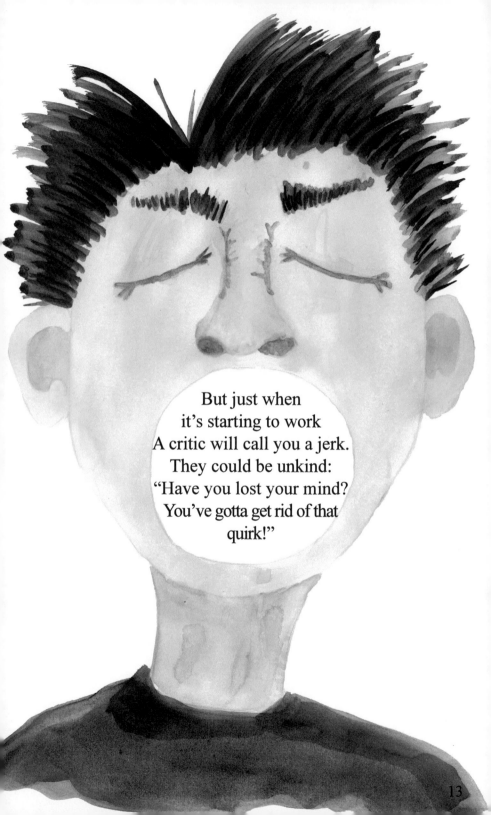

But just when
it's starting to work
A critic will call you a jerk.
They could be unkind:
"Have you lost your mind?
You've gotta get rid of that
quirk!"

13

You might want to watch who you tell
Since some will be eager to quell
Your new-found delight.
They could be uptight.
No way do we want a hard sell!

At first, just like me, you may find
To do what you want seems unkind.
To hear you say NO
Could seem like a blow
And might make you think that they mind.

So now it begins to get tricky
And may even seem a bit sticky.
For you to be free
As you need to be,
Could certainly seem to them icky!

And here it comes down to a choice:
Please others; or find your own voice.
THEY'LL say it's the worst
To put yourself first
But you'll just bliss out and rejoice!

How much do you want this new thing?
You know why I'm now the YOUNG Ing?
I wanted more fun
To be not all done.
I wanted to have one last fling!

To heck with the old age convention
No way I had any intention
To act my own age.
So to take center stage
I planned to create an invention!

And here's where it starts to get funny.
Whatever I touched turned to honey.
I'd say what I want;
My virtues I'd flaunt.
And in rolled great barrels of money!

My new life was just such a blast
I had to make sure it would last.
So then I began
To make a bold plan
And put it in place really fast.

My plan was quite simple and clear,
Not just to get young year by year.
That might take too long.
I could be long gone.
I wanted it now and right here!

I took a good look at my face.
I needed to slow down this race;
—Get quite free of TIME
—Turn round on a dime
And then I could go at MY pace.

I wanted my face to reflect
The years that I chose to reject
And so I sought signs
Of lots fewer lines
And that I began to detect.

The very first thing that I spied
Made gurus strike out as a guide:
"Cracked nails come with age."
That's not on MY page
I sent that one out with the tide!

I pictured nails strong as a brick
And this simple shift did the trick.
My life to enhance
I gave youth a chance.
The changes I got were quite quick!

I found more and more younging signs.
Got rid of some unwanted lines,
A sigh of relief!
A brand new belief!
I'd gotten new wine from old vines!

For when we can find evidence
No longer just sit on the fence.
We then have the guts
Who cares if we're "nuts?"
The pay-off for us is immense!

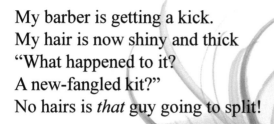

My barber is getting a kick.
My hair is now shiny and thick
"What happened to it?
A new-fangled kit?"
No hairs is *that* guy going to split!

You want all the help you can get
To get to your goal on a jet.
So when your FRIENDS say;
"You sparkle today!"
Believe them! It helps you stay set!

When others acknowledge the feat
That really does feel pretty neat.
Let's throw out the old!
Let's bring in the bold!
No way will we take a back seat!

And that is the merry-go-round
To get yourself up on high ground.
Reverse the decay.
See progress each day,
And more happy feelings abound!

As long as you keep feeling old
Your younging is out in the cold.
We've said it before.
We'll say it once more:
To think and feel young's solid gold.

We're going for energy here!
The zest of a true pioneer!
To fill up your cup,
Just start to look up.
Feel juiced and alive ear to ear!

Let's just start to see what this means
We've stamina worthy of teens!
With every new dish
Life gets more delish
And we can fit into our jeans!

There's nothing we can't be or do!
This ball game called life is brand new!
We've turned back the clock,
We're startin' to rock!
We're with it! - The current Who's Who!

Last night I got ten hours sleep.
I sprang from my bed with a leap!
The smooth skin of tots?
It's not from kumquats.
It's 'cuz of the hours they keep!

I've got a new take on Van Winkle
He must have had nary a wrinkle!
A forty-year sleep?
That's gotta be deep!
I bet his eye had a big twinkle!

21

"Young, what do I do with the thought
And this one comes rather a lot,
That it can't be done
Not under the sun
And in this sad thought I feel caught?"

A very good question indeed!
Each one of us has a strong need
To banish the doubt,
To turn it about
And quickly return to our creed.

For as my adventure began,
To be my own number 1 fan:
To sing my own praises,
I saw how that fazes
The teachings of many a clan.

To dump so-called wisdom of sages
Passed on to me down through the ages
To sing my own praises
I needed new phrases
They had to be strong and outrageous.

I started my own catalogue
Of virtues I wrote in a log.
Was it real lilty?
Did I feel guilty?
I did, but pulled out of the fog.

Whenever you harbor a doubt
You need to get that puppy out!
You need a belief
To give you relief;
—A grab bag of thoughts that have clout.

I can change my thoughts!

I can change my words!

I can change my mind!

So when such a thought strikes you next
Remember the theme of our text
I WANT TO FEEL GOOD!
I WANT TO FEEL GOOD!
Be happy! No need to feel vexed!

Be grateful! Just answer *that* call!
Be grateful and you'll have a ball!
When you can change hateful
To funny and grateful
You'll feel good in no time at all!

So let us begin once again
To help you believe that you can.
Just see yourself now
The new youthful wow
As peppy as when you were 10!

Now if that's a stretch for today
No matter! It's really okay.
Tomorrow will do.
What's one day or two?
The fun's getting into the fray.

And pay no attention to those
Whose hearts lost their courage and froze.
They've lost all their zest
-Seek nothing but rest
Just wanting to sit and to doze.

Our world is so steeped in the Nays.
Could that be what speeds up the haze?
If that be the case
Small wonder our race
Seems doomed to be stuck in its ways.

Who wants to be part of *that* scene?
There's no way we want to be mean.
Dissing our body
Thinking it's shoddy,
Just love it and help it get lean!

Your body's not rigid, it's flowing,
It's ever renewing and glowing.
So when you feel pain
Just sing this refrain:
"This twinge means it's younger I'm growing."

To ramp up your rate of belief
You need to turn up a new leaf.
So here are some facts
To let you relax.
And breathe a big sigh of relief!

I know this will make you feel gay.
We've tons of new cells every day,
Repairing our skin.
That's how we can win.
Come on golden oldies, let's play!

"If each day my cells are brand new
Then each day should I feel new too?"
New cells you have got.
New thoughts you have not.
New cells with old thoughts just won't do!

Your body responds to your mind
So find the best thought you can find:
-Your cells will renew
'Cuz that's what cells do
When you become gentle and kind.

"So, tell me Young Ing, is it true
That thinking is all I need do?
Why that is such fun
Consider it done
Before you can count up to two."

Well, thinking is surely one part
And would be a good place to start
Then notice your feeling.
If it sends you reeling
Find one that comes straight from your heart.

The body will surely respond
To thoughts like a magical wand
"My body is aging."
Will send your cells raging
And make them feel totally conned.

Since how you are feeling's a clue
To feel good will work for you too.
So just be alert
And you'll hit pay dirt.
Your body'll look and feel new.

And when you feel bad, don't despair.
Just do a wee tweak here or there.
Go out for a walk
To hear the birds talk
Or go and relax in a chair.

Remember there's no one to blame
If many sad feelings remain.
Don't see a result?
No reason to pout!
Just follow the rules of our game.

And Rule Number 1 is have fun
The fun is that it's never done!
A nice soothing bath
Keeps you on your path
Reminding you that you've begun!

My body's become my best friend.
It now loves to wiggle and bend.
When it hears a beat
It turns up the heat.
I think it's begun a new trend!

Let *your* body know it's adored.
From now on it won't be ignored.
Your cells you can soothe.
Your skin can feel smooth.
Your mind will no longer be bored!

Imagine you're down by a brook.
You see there how you want to look.
You're dressed to the nines!
No wrinkles or lines!
Page 1 in your new Younging book.

So what if it isn't too late
To totally master your fate,
For you to control
Your body and soul?
What fantasies would you create?

Now is it a puzzle to pick
The things that would give you a kick?
Make your heart sing?
Give your life zing?
Get you up in the morning real quick?

Just how would you follow your dreams?
Meander down some foreign streams?
Sail into a port?
Take up a new sport?
Be featured on one of those teams?

I wake up each morning and say:
"I want to have great fun to-day!"
I follow my bliss
By blowing a kiss
And keep feeling happy and gay.

What brings me the most joy by far
Is strumming notes on my guitar.
I may sing along
If I like the song.
If not, I'll go out and shoot par.

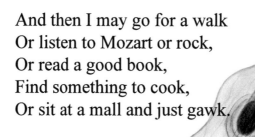

And then I may go for a walk
Or listen to Mozart or rock,
Or read a good book,
Find something to cook,
Or sit at a mall and just gawk.

It could be there's something to buy,
Perhaps a neat puzzle to try.
The most fun for me
Is what's new to see.
That gives me a beautiful high!

So when *you're* young what will it be?
What new things do *you* want to see?
Something outrageous?
Maybe contagious?
Infecting the world with great glee?

 We're looking to laugh and have fun
By putting the blues on the run.
How awesome is that?
To be where it's at?
In no time this age game is won!

"It's not hard to laugh and have fun
When you've got the blues on the run.
But when you feel punk
And in a big funk
Then, how in the heck is it done?"

For starters, a low mood to dump
Try taking a hop, skip   and jump.
This sounds so absurd
It might not occur
To anyone deep in a slump.

And when you are feeling insane
You want to get rid of the pain
Just write a short verse
Without a rehearse
Then go for a walk in the rain.

Start thinking of things that you like.
How long since you've ridden a bike?
Two-wheel or three-wheel
Not *that* big a deal.
Had fun with a tyke on a trike?

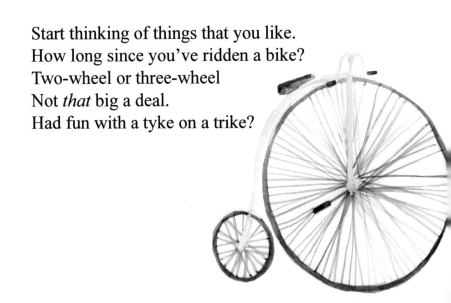

Be playful! No need to try hard.
Feel good! Play your new laughter card!
Just *your* self to please
With comfort and ease
Right here in your very own yard.

You don't even have to leave home
You might want to knock off a poem.
If traveling's your thing
Your heart can go zing!
Just do it! Go buzz off to Rome!

Come on with me down to the park
I think we'll be there before dark
We'll swing on a swing
A round twirly thing.
What fun! What a blast! What a lark!

Suppose that it's all up to you
That you're free to do or not do.
You're running this ship
You soar or you dip
The skipper is you—only you!

So let yourself sit and relax.
No need that your logic be taxed
No hocus pocus!
Just about focus
On one or two clear simple facts.

It's never too late to have fun.
This thought keeps the blues on the run.
This moment's brand new
And waiting for you
To savor the trip you've begun.

To feel this good younging is sweet
Just try it! You'll savor a treat!
You surely weren't born
Your body to scorn
By letting it get old and beat!

Come drink from the fountain of youth!
A lot bigger buzz than vermouth!
You'll just have more fun!
You'll never be done.
And that's not too far from the truth!

I know you are loving this song.
You wouldn't have stayed here so long
If you hadn't felt
The hand you've been dealt
Holds more than you've played all along.

You want to be all you can be
I think that you now have the key
Control how you feel
With humor and zeal
And you'll see how that sets you free!

We've come to the end of the page.
We've beautifully set up the stage.
When you only do
What's most fun for you
You'll feel, look and act your new age!

There is a Young person called Ing
Whose age is a wonderful thing.
And yours will be too
When you only do
What feels good and makes your heart sing!

THE END

43